Air Fryer Cookbook For Young Chefs

AIR FRYER
COOKBOOK
FOR YOUNG
CHEFS

Enjoy The Flavours Of Effortless Healthy Recipes You Love To Eat

Jennifer Seal

TABLE OF CONTENTS
INTRODUCTION

INTRODUCTION

Do you know that a chef is a skilled professional who is engaged in preparing food, often leading a kitchen or culinary team? They are a specialized group trained in various cooking techniques and oversee the creation of dishes, managing the kitchen operations and ensuring high-quality meals. It is awesome that we are adventuring into this great discipline which at the end of the day will produce young great achievers in kitchen mastery.

Catch them young and teach them how to do it. Good knowledge acquired is not a waste. It is an invaluable tool. Let the kids learn how to do it when you are not there. Teach them what they need to know earlier.

There are a lot of juvenile delinquencies today as a result of some parental deficiencies. So parents, uncle, aunts, guardians let's get into the job!The kids can do it, even better!-Jennifer Seal.

Welcome to the exciting world of culinary adventures! The "Air Fryer Cookbook for Young Chefs" is your gateway to discovering the magic of creating delicious, healthy meals using the innovative air fryer. Packed with easy-to-follow recipes and creative cooking techniques, this book is designed to empower young chefs to unleash their culinary talents while exploring a world of flavorful possibilities. Whether you are a beginner or a budding kitchen maestro, get ready to embark on a flavorful journey that will elevate your cooking skills and delight your taste buds!

THE PURPOSE OF THIS BOOK

These are few reasons why this book,Air Fryer Cookbook For Young Chefs " was published.

1-Promoting Healthy Eating: To teach kids about healthier alternatives and encourage them to make nutritious choices using the air fryer.

2-Building Confidence: This book will facilitate the instilling of confidence in young chefs by providing step-by-step instructions for delicious recipes, empowering them to explore cooking independently.

3-Developing Culinary Skills: Help kids learn fundamental cooking skills like measuring ingredients, understanding cooking times, and experimenting with flavours in a safe and fun way.

4-Encouraging Creativity:. Inspire creativity by including recipes that allow for personalization and experimentation, fostering a love for cooking beyond following instructions.

5-Family Bonding: Create opportunities for kids and families to cook together, fostering stronger bonds and creating lasting memories through shared cooking experiences.

6-Cultural Exploration: Introduce diverse cuisines and dishes from around the world, sparking curiosity and appreciation for different cultures through food.

7-Emphasizing Safety: Teach kitchen safety practices tailored to kids, ensuring they understand the importance of being cautious and responsible while cooking.

This book is designed to build young kids up in the acquisition of culinary mastery. At the end of this enlightenment through this book, the young chefs are expected to know their way about in the kitchen:

1- They must have learnt the guidelines on how to get started with the kitchen appliances, how to operate the air fryer and other kitchen equipment.

2-They should also have acquired the knowledge of the benefits of using the air fryer and the step by step guide in selecting the proper recipes for the machine and how to prepare them.

3- This book will enable them to embrace the culture of self consciousness, doing it well when the adults are not there. They must have mastered the maintenance of the air fryer and other kitchen devices.

"Air Fryer Cookbook For Young Chefs" will empower your kids with the excitement and love for kitchen mastery. It is a book that must be on their bookshelf.

WHAT IS AN AIR FRYER?

An air fryer is a kitchen appliance that uses hot air circulation to cook food,providing a healthier alternative to traditional frying methods. It typically consists of a basket or tray where the food is placed, and a heating element and fan that circulate hot air around the food at high speed.The machine cooks the food by producing a crisp layer on the outside, similar to frying, using significantly less oil or sometimes none at all. The rapid hot air circulation creates a crispy texture while cooking the food thoroughly.

Air fryers are versatile and can cook a wide variety of foods,not limited to fries, chicken wings, vegetables, fish, and even desserts. They often come with temperature controls and timers, allowing users to adjust settings for different types of food. The cooking process tends to be faster than traditional methods, making it convenient for quick meals.

As a young chef,the air fryer provides you a convenient way to enjoy crispy and delicious foods with less oil,

making them a popular choice for health-conscious persons
looking forward to indulging in fried foods in a healthier manner.

HOW TO USE THIS BOOK

An air fryer cookbook for young chefs can be a fun and useful tool in the kitchen. Here is a breakdown of the step by step guide for using it:

*__Introduction__: Start by reading the introduction or first few pages. Often, the introduction gives an overview of the air fryer, its benefits, and tips for using it safely and effectively.

*__Recipes:__ The cookbook will likely have a variety of recipes categorized by meals (breakfast, lunch, dinner, snacks, desserts). Browse through the contents and select a recipe that interests you.

*__Ingredients and Equipment:__ Check the list of ingredients required for the chosen recipe. Make sure you have everything on hand. Also, review. the equipment needed, such as specific air fryer accessories or utensils.

*__Instructions__: Read the recipe instructions carefully before starting. Air fryers can have different settings and temperatures, so for you to
understand the steps involved is crucial for a successful outcome.

*__Ingredients__: Gather and prepare all the ingredients according to the recipe necessary for each meal.

*__Preheat the Air Fryer:__ Some recipes might require preheating the air fryer. Follow the instructions in the cookbook to set the correct
temperature.

*__Cooking:__ Place the prepared ingredients into the air fryer basket or trays as directed. Set the cooking time and temperature according to the recipe.

*__Monitor:__ Keep an eye on the cooking process through the air fryer's window or by occasionally checking the food.

*__Serve__: Once the food is cooked, carefully remove it from the air fryer. Follow any additional
instructions in the cookbook for serving or garnishing.

*<u>Experiment</u>:Feel free to experiment with the recipes once you're comfortable. Adjust cooking times, temperatures, or ingredients to suit your taste.Remember, the cookbook is a guide, and cooking often involves personal preferences.

Do not hesitate to modify recipes to better suit your choice. And most importantly, have fun exploring new dishes with your airfryer.

CHAPTER ONE
UNDERSTANDING YOUR AIR FRYER

Understanding your air fryer is a very crucial aspect of this book, for safe and effective cooking. Before embarking on using the air fryer machine, consider the following factors:.

1.Components:
You need to get yourself familiarized with the components of the machine, the basket or tray, the heating element, fan, temperature controls, and other settings specific to your model. Failure to implement this, can generate a household accident, loss of your cooking recipes and ingredients or more so, cause a technical fault to the device. Ensure that you are acquainted with the operations of the air fryer machine before use.

2.Functionality:
Know how the air fryer works. It circulates hot air around the food, providing a crispy texture similar to frying but using minimal or no oil.

3.**Temperature** **And Time**: Understand the temperature and time settings. Different foods require varying temperatures and durations for optimal cooking. Experimentation and following recipes methods help in understanding this better.

4.**Preheating**:
Some air fryers require preheating before use. Follow the manufacturer's instructions for preheating times.

5.**Cooking Capacities**: Learn the cooking capacity of your air fryer. Overcrowding the basket can hinder proper airflow, resulting in unevenly cooked food. Put the adequate size of meal for a particular cooking. When you are cooking for one,the planning is different from a family or friends'meal.

6. **Cooking Techniques:** Understand different cooking techniques; frying, roasting,baking, and others. Your air fryer can perform multiple functions; explore recipes and techniques to utilize its versatility. Avoid using an air fryer on presumptions.

7. **Healthier Cooking:** Emphasize the health benefits of using an air fryer; it requires less oil compared to traditional frying, reducing overall fat intake while still offering a crispy texture.

8.Safety Features: Be aware of any safety features your air fryer might have,such as auto-shutdown mechanisms or overheating protection.This knowledge ensures safer operation.

9.**Maintenance:** Regular cleaning and maintenance are essential for optimal performance.Learn how to properly disassemble and clean the components. Some parts might be dishwasher-safe, but always check the manual. Always wash the parts that are washable before and after use. This will help prevent lingering odours of old foods on the devices which can affect the flavour of your new recipes. Always clean your air fryer machine with hot soapy water and rinse and dry for another meal. Do not use an air fryer when it is faulty. When white smoke starts coming out of the air fryer,it is an indication that there is too much fat in your recipe which drops oil into the machine. This can easily be fixed by cleaning up the underneath fryer basket before you continue. Also,if black smoke is seen,it is a sign that the machine is faulty. In that case,you should unplug the machine and take it to the repairer.

10.**Recipe Adaptations:.** Adapt your favourite recipes for the air fryer. Experiment with different foods and cooking times to achieve the desired results.

11.**Troubleshooting:**Understand some basic

troubleshooting techniques for common issues such as uneven cooking, strange odours, or malfunctioning controls. Refer to the manual for guidance.

12-**Experimentations:** Finally, do not be afraid to experiment! Try various recipes and food types to get a feel for what works best in your air fryer. Learning comes through practice. As a young chef,the understanding of these aspects will enable you to harness the full potential of your air fryer, ensuring safe and delightful culinary experiences.

ESSENTIAL TOOLS

These tools and accessories listed in this chapter, can make cooking with your air fryer machine more efficient,versatile,and enjoyable. Adjust any based on your specific cooking preference and recipes you plan to explore.

SILICONE TONGS OR UTENSILS

Silicone tongs are kitchen utensils with two arms joined by a hinge and operated with a spring mechanism or a lock. They are made primarily from silicone, a heat-resistant and non-stick material. Here's an in-depth look at their uses and maintenance:

Uses:
Handling Hot Food: Silicone tongs are ideal for gripping and flipping hot food items in the air fryer or on the stovetop without scratching surfaces or damaging coatings.

Versatile Cooking Tool: They are versatile for various cooking tasks - from flipping meat on a grill to serving salads, pasta, or vegetables.
Non-stick Surface: The silicone surface prevents scratching on non-stick cookware and ensures easy release of food.

Maintenance:

1–Cleaning: They are dishwasher-safe but can also be easily cleaned by hand. Use mild dish soap and warm water to remove grease or residue.

2–Heat Resistance: Silicone tongs are heat-resistant, generally safe to use at high temperatures. However, excessive heat exposure might degrade them over time.

3–Avoid Sharp Objects: While silicone is durable, it is not completely resistant to cuts or punctures from sharp objects. Avoid using them to handle extremely sharp or rough-edged items.

4–Storage: Store silicone tongs in a dry area to prevent moisture build-up. Hanging them or keeping them in a utensil drawer with other kitchen tools can help maintain their shape.

5–Inspect Regularly: Check for any signs of wear and tear, such as cracks or damage to the silicone surface. If you notice any, consider replacing them to ensure safety during use.

6–Avoid Direct Flame: Silicone tongs should not be exposed to direct flames as it can cause damage even though it is heat resistant.

Benefits:

1-Heat Resistance: Silicone tongs can withstand high temperatures, making them suitable for cooking without risk of melting or warping.

2-Non-Stick Properties: They are gentle on surfaces and can not scratch or damage non-stick cookware or air fryer baskets.

3-Hygienic: Silicone is easy to clean and does not harbour bacteria or odours.
Silicone tongs are an essential kitchen tool for handling hot food and offer convenience and versatility. Proper maintenance ensures their longevity and continued safe use in the kitchen.

OIL SPRAY BOTTLE OR MISTING SPRAYER

An oil spray bottle is handy for air frying as it allows you to evenly distribute a thin layer of oil on food, promoting a crispy texture. To maintain it, rinse it thoroughly after each use, avoid using thick oils that can clog the sprayer, and periodically clean it with warm, soapy water to prevent residue buildup. Regularly check and clean the nozzle to ensure it sprays properly.

PARCHMENT PAPER OR PERFORATED LINERS

An air fryer perforated liner or parchment paper is used to line the air fryer basket, preventing food from sticking to the basket while allowing air to circulate for even cooking. The liner or parchment paper typically has perforations to facilitate airflow, ensuring your food gets crispy without sticking to the basket. It is a convenient way to make cleanup easier and helps maintain the air fryer's non-stick coating.To maintain an air fryer perforated liner or parchment paper, dispose of any food debris after each use. If using parchment paper, ensure it doesn't cover the entire basket to allow proper airflow. For reusable liners, wash them with warm, soapy water after use, and if they're dishwasher-safe, you can use the dishwasher for cleaning. Store them flat or loosely rolled to prevent creases or damage. Regularly inspect for any tears or damage and replace if needed to maintain their effectiveness.

KITCHEN THERMOMETER

A kitchen thermometer is a tool used to measure the internal temperature of food accurately. It ensures that meat, poultry, fish, and other dishes are cooked to a safe temperature, minimizing the risk of foodborne illnesses. There are various types, such as instant-read, probe, and infrared thermometers, each suitable for specific purposes.

Maintenance

This involves cleaning the thermometer after each use, following the manufacturer's instructions. Many are water-resistant and can be gently washed by hand with soap and water. Be cautious with probe thermometers not to immerse the entire device in water if it's not waterproof. Store them properly and calibrate them periodically to ensure accuracy, as some may drift over time. Regularly check for any signs of damage or wear and replace if needed.

RACK OR MULTIPLAYER COOKING INSERT

An air fryer rack is an accessory designed for use inside an air fryer basket. It is typically a metal rack with legs that elevates food, allowing hot air to circulate evenly around it. This accessory enables you to cook multiple items simultaneously or cook foods that might benefit from being raised closer to the heat source, promoting even crisping.

Maintaining an air fryer rack involves cleaning it after each use. Depending on the material, it can usually be washed with warm, soapy water by hand or placed in the dishwasher if it is dishwasher-safe. Ensure it is completely dry before storing it to prevent rust or corrosion. Inspect it regularly for any signs of damage, such as warping or bending, and replace it if necessary to maintain its functionality and safety.

MEAT TENDERIZER

MALLET

A meat tenderizer is a tool used to break down the filaments in tougher cuts of meat, making them more tender and easier to bite . It can come in colourful forms, similar as mallets with textured shells or needle-suchlike bias.

Uses:

Softening tough cuts- Helps to tenderize and flatten tougher cuts of meat like steaks, chops, or flesh. Indeed cooking By levelling flesh, it promotes more invariant cuisine, reducing   cuisine time for thicker cuts. conservation drawing Wash it completely after each use, either by hand or in the dishwasher, depending on the material.

Storage

Store in a dry place to help rust or damage. Some may come with covers for the sharp edges to insure safety. Check for damage Periodically check for any signs of damage or wear, especially if it is a mallet with a texturedsurface.However, consider replacing it to avoid impurity or injury during use, If it becomes worn or damaged.

BAKING PAN OR SILICONE

A baking pan is a metal or glass container used for baking various foods like cakes, cookies, and more. Silicone baking pans are made from flexible silicone material.

Uses:

1;Baking cakes, cookies, brownies, and other baked goods. Roasting vegetables or meats. 2-Making frozen treats like ice cubes or popsicles.

Maintenance:

For metal or glass pans, hand wash with mild soap and water. Avoid using abrasive scrubbers to prevent damage to the surface. Silicone pans are usually dishwasher safe but check the manufacturer's instructions to be sure. Ensure thorough drying after washing to prevent water spots or rusting (for metal pans).

Store in a dry place to prevent any mould or mildew growth on silicone pans.

For both types, avoid using sharp utensils that could scratch the surface and impact their longevity.

GRILL PAN OR SKEWERS

A grill pan is a stovetop pan with raised ridges designed to mimic the cooking effect of an outdoor grill. Skewers are long, thin metal or wooden rods used to thread and cook food, especially meats and vegetables.

Uses:

Grill pans are ideal for indoor grilling, providing grill-like sear marks on meats, vegetables, and even sandwiches. Skewers are perfect for making kebabs or skewered meats and vegetables, allowing for easy flipping and even cooking.

Maintenance:

1–Grill pans should be hand washed with mild soap and water, using a non-abrasive sponge or cloth to clean the ridges

2-.Seasoning the grill pan occasionally with oil helps maintain its non-stick properties and prevents rust.

3-Skewers should be cleaned thoroughly after each use to remove any food residue. Soaking wooden skewers before use prevents them from burning during cooking.

4-Store grill pans and skewers in a dry area to prevent rust or moisture damage

Regular cleaning and proper storage enhance the longevity of both grill pans and skewers.

FOOD BRUSH

A food brush, commonly known as a basting brush, is a kitchen utensil used for applying sauces, marinades, oils, or melted butter onto food during cooking or grilling.

Uses;

This tool is used in applying sauces, marinades, or oil onto meats, fish, vegetables, or baked goods.

Basting food to keep it moist and add flavour during cooking. Also for glazing pastries or bread with egg wash or melted butter.

Maintenance:

1-Wash the food brush with warm, soapy water after each use to remove any residue.

2-For silicone or nylon brushes, they are often dishwasher safe, but refer to the manufacturer's instructions.

3-Natural bristle brushes should be cleaned thoroughly and air-dried to prevent bacterial growth.

4-Store the brush in a clean, dry place to avoid any odours or contamination. Regularly cleaning and proper drying help maintain the hygiene of the food brush and extend its lifespan.

AN AIR FRYER COOKBOOK

An air fryer cookbook is a guide filled with recipes specifically tailored for cooking with an air fryer. Its uses include:

1-Recipe Variety: It offers a wide range of recipes, from appetizers to main courses and desserts, all adapted for air frying. Instructions:

Provides detailed instructions on how to use an air fryer effectively, including temperature settings, cooking times, and techniques unique to air frying.

2-Cooking Tips: Offers tips and tricks for getting the best results from your air fryer, such as how to properly coat foods with oil or seasoning for optimal taste and texture.

3-Healthy Cooking: Focuses on healthier alternatives to traditionally fried foods, emphasizing lower fat content and reduced oil usage.

4-Inspiration: Inspires creativity by suggesting new dishes and innovative ways to use the air fryer beyond the typical fried foods, including baking, roasting, and grilling.

An air fryer cookbook serves as a valuable resource for both beginners and experienced users, enhancing the cooking experience with this versatile kitchen appliance.

OVEN MITTS OR SILICONE

GRIPS

Oven mitts and silicone oven gloves are heat-resistant kitchen accessories used to protect hands and arms while handling hot cookware and bakeware.

Uses:

1– For handling hot pots, pans, baking sheets, and dishes from the oven or stovetop.

2–Gripping and manoeuvring hot grilling tools or barbecue equipment. Safely removing items from the microwave or handling hot items during food preparation.

Maintenance:

Oven mitts made of fabric are generally machine washable. Follow the care instructions provided by the manufacturer. Silicone oven gloves can usually be washed by hand with soap and water, and some are also dishwasher safe. Allow mitts or gloves to air dry thoroughly before storing.Check for any signs of wear, tear, or heat damage regularly, and replace them if they show signs of deterioration to maintain safety. Regular cleaning and inspecting for damage are important to ensure proper protection against heat and maintain the longevity of oven mitts or silicone gloves.

FOOD PREP TOOLS

Food prep tools are essential in the kitchen for various tasks involved in preparing ingredients before cooking. Some common prep tools include:

1–Chef's Knife: Used for chopping, slicing, and dicing a wide variety of ingredients like vegetables, fruits, and meats.

2–Cutting Board: Provides a safe surface for chopping and cutting ingredients. Wooden and plastic boards should be washed with soap and water after each use.

3-Vegetable Peeler: For peeling skins off vegetables and fruits. Wash with soap and water after use.

4–Box Grater: Used for grating cheese, vegetables, and other foods. Clean with a brush and soap after use.

5–Measuring Spoons and Cups: Essential for accurately measuring ingredients. Wash with soap and water after use.

6–Mixing Bowls: For combining ingredients. Dishwashers are safe in most cases, but hand washing is recommended to maintain their quality.

7–Colander or Strainer: Used to drain liquids from foods. Wash with soap and water after each use.

Maintenance

Wash all tools thoroughly with soap and water after each use to prevent bacterial growth and food residue buildup. For some tools, such as knives and graters, extra care is needed to prevent accidents. Store them properly in a safe place to avoid injuries and maintain their sharpness. Avoid soaking wooden tools for extended periods; instead, wipe them clean and dry them immediately after use to prevent warping or cracking. Proper maintenance and regular cleaning ensure that prep tools remain safe to use and last longer in the kitchen.

CLEANING TOOLS

Cleaning tools are indispensable in maintaining a tidy and hygienic kitchen environment. Here's a detailed note on various cleaning tools and their maintenance:.

1-Sponges andScrubbers:

Sponges are versatile for general cleaning tasks, while scrubbers are useful for tougher stains and residues. Rinse thoroughly after each use, allow them to air dry, and sanitize sponges regularly by microwaving damp sponges for a minute or soaking them in a bleach solution.Replace sponges and scrubbers regularly to prevent bacterial growth.

2–Dish Brushes and Bottle Brushes: Dish brushes are excellent for washing dishes, pots, and pans, while bottle brushes are ideal for cleaning narrow-necked containers.

Rinse and air dry after each use, and replace brushes periodically to avoid accumulation of food particles and bacteria.

3–Dishcloths and Towels: Dishcloths and kitchen towels are used for drying dishes and wiping countertops.Launder dishcloths and towels frequently in hot water with detergent to remove germs and food residues

4-Mop and Broom:

Mops are for cleaning floors, while brooms are used for sweeping.Rinse and air dry the mop after use. Clean broom bristles regularly by shaking or tapping them against a hard surface.

5-Vacuum Cleaner:

Useful for cleaning up larger debris or crumbs from floors.Empty the vacuum cleaner bag or container regularly and. clean the filters to maintain suction power.

6-Cleaning Solutions:

Use appropriate cleaning solutions for different surfaces (e.g., multipurpose cleaners, glass cleaners, disinfectants) Follow instructions on the product label for correct usage and dilution.

7-Gloves:

Rubber gloves protect hands while using cleaning chemicals or hot water.   Rinse gloves thoroughly after use and   allow them to air dry completely.

Maintenance Tips

Rinse and clean cleaning tools thoroughly after each use to prevent the growth of bacteria and odours. Allow tools to air dry completely before storing to avoid mould and mildew.

Regularly replace worn-out or damaged cleaning tools to maintain   their   effectiveness. Follow manufacturer instructions for specific cleaning tools, especially regarding washing and maintenance guidelines. Proper care and maintenance of cleaning tools ensure their longevity and efficiency in keeping the kitchen clean and sanitized.

VEGETABLE PEELER OR SPIRALIZER

A vegetable peeler and a spiralizer are two kitchen tools used for preparing vegetables, each with its unique functions.

Vegetable Peeler:

Uses:

It is used for peeling the skin off vegetables and fruits like potatoes, carrots, apples, and cucumbers. Creating thin slices or ribbons of vegetables for salads, garnishes, or recipes requiring thinly sliced veggies. Removing imperfections or blemishes from produce.

Maintenance:

Wash the vegetable peeler with warm, soapy water after each use. For some peelers, cleaning can be done in a dishwasher, but it's advisable to check the manufacturer's instructions. Ensure the peeler is completely dry before storing to prevent rusting. Store it in a safe place to avoid damage to the blade.

Spiralizer:

Uses:

Creating vegetable noodles or "zoodles" from vegetables like zucchini, carrots, and squash for healthier pasta alternatives. Making curly fries, salads, or garnishes using spiral-cut vegetables. Providing various blade options for different cuts (noodles, ribbons, spirals).

Maintenance:

Disassemble the spiralizer and wash the parts with warm, soapy water after each use. Some parts might be dishwasher safe. Use a brush to clean hard-to-reach places or food residues. Ensure thorough drying before reassembling or storing to prevent mould or rust. Store the spiralizer in a dry place, keeping the blades safely stored to avoid accidental cuts. Regular cleaning and proper storage of both the vegetable peeler and spiralizer are essential to maintain their hygiene and extend their lifespan, ensuring they remain effective in food preparation.

SAFETY TIPS FOR YOUNG CHEF

Below are some safety tips for young chefs who are starting off to use an air fryer. It is very risky to allow underaged kids to use appliances that they are not knowledgeable about. Ihe result of engaging in it can be disastrous. This book offers guidelines on the dos and don'ts while using an air fryer as a young chef.

1.Read the Manual:

Always start by reading the manufacturer's manual thoroughly. Understand the specific functionalities, warnings, and safety precautions for your particular air fryer model.

2. Location & Surface:

Place the air fryer on a stable, heat-resistant surface away from walls, cabinets, and other appliances. Ensure there is enough space around it for proper ventilation. Keep it away from flammable materials like polythene ,bags.rubber made utensils, to avoid catching fire as a result of the intense heat from the air fryer.

3. Preheat with Care:.

Preheat the air fryer as instructed in the manual but be cautious while handling the hot components. Use oven mitts or silicone grips when necessary.

4. Use Proper Utensils:

Use non-metallic utensils to avoid damaging the air fryer's basket and interior coating. Wooden or silicone utensils are good choices.

5. Avoid Overfilling:

Do not overfill the basket with food. Follow the recommended guidelines to prevent overcrowding, ensuring proper air circulation for every cooking.

6. Check for Moisture:

Pat dry the food items to minimize excess moisture, as this can cause splattering or even accidents due to the release of steam.

7. Monitor Cooking:

Regularly check on the food during the cooking process. This helps prevent overcooking or potential burning. Avoid anything that will distract your attention when you are getting your meal done using an air fryer.

8. Avoid Aerosol Sprays:

Refrain from using aerosol sprays directly on the air fryer basket, as these can damage the non-stick coating.

9. Careful Removal:

When the cooking cycle is finished, use caution when removing the basket or trays, as they might be hot. Use proper handling tools like oven mitts. Always allow the air fryer to cool down before cleaning. Follow the manufacturer's instructions for proper maintenance and cleaning of the appliance.

10. Unplug When Not in Use:

After use, unplug the air fryer and let it cool completely before storing it away.   Encourage them to take their time and understand the device thoroughly for a safe and enjoyable cooking experience.

CHAPTER TWO

EASY SNACKS AND APPERTIZER

1–CRUNCHY VEGGIE CHIPS
Ingredient

*Assorted vegetables (such as sweet potatoes, beets, zucchini, carrot.

*Olive oil or cooking spray

*Salt, pepper, or seasoning of choice (optional)
Instructions:
Preparation: Preheat the air fryer to the recommended temperature for vegetable chips (usually around 350°F/180°C).

Prepare Vegetables:

Wash and dry the vegetables thoroughly. Slice the vegetables thinly and uniformly using a knife or a mandoline slicer. This ensures even cooking.

Seasoning: Toss the sliced vegetables in a bowl with a drizzle of olive oil or lightly spray them with cooking spray for a crispy texture.

Add salt, pepper, or any preferred seasoning to taste. (Optional: Use spices like paprika, garlic powder, or herbs for added flavour.)

Air Frying:

Arrange the seasoned vegetable slices in a single layer in the air fryer basket or tray. Avoid overcrowding to ensure proper crisping. Cook for about 8-12 minutes, flipping the chips halfway through the cooking time for even browning. Cooking time may vary based on the thickness of the slices and the air fryer model.Keep an eye on the chips and remove them when they turn crispy and golden brown. Some may cook faster than others, so remove individual chips as they finish cooking.

Serving:

Let the chips cool for a few minutes to crisp up further before serving.

Enjoy the crunchy veggie chips as a healthy snack or appetizer.

Nutritional Values (per serving)

This may vary based on vegetables used and portion size):

1—Calories: Varies based on the vegetable type and portion size (typically around 50-100 calories per serving).

2—Fat: Depends on the amount of oil used for cooking.

3—Carbohydrates: Varies but generally lower compared to traditional potato chips.

4—Fibre: Good source of dietary fibre

5—Vitamins and Minerals: Rich in vitamins A, C, and K, as well as minerals like potassium and manganese from different vegetables.

These veggie chips offer a nutritious alternative to store-bought chips, packed with vitamins, minerals, and fibre while satisfying the craving for a crunchy snack. Adjust seasonings and cooking times based on personal preferences and experiment with different vegetables for diverse flavours and textures.

2–MOZZARELLA STICKS

Mozzarella sticks are a beloved appetizer or snack made from mozzarella cheese coated in breadcrumbs and fried until golden and crispy. They are often served with marinara sauce for dipping, offering a delightful combination of gooey, melted cheese encased in a crunchy exterior.

Mode of Preparation:

Ingredients:

Mozzarella cheese (low-moisture)
Breadcrumbs Eggs
Flour Seasonings
(like salt, pepper, garlic powder)
Oil for frying

Marinara sauce for serving

Preparation Steps:

Cut the mozzarella into stick-shaped pieces. Prepare a breading station: one bowl with flour, another with beaten eggs, and a third with breadcrumbs mixed with seasonings.   Coat each mozzarella stick in flour, then dip it in the egg mixture, and finally coat it thoroughly with breadcrumbs.

Repeat the coating process (flour, egg, breadcrumbs) for a thicker crust if desired.   Place the coated sticks on a baking sheet and freeze them for about 30 minutes to firm up.

Heat oil in a deep pan or fryer to about 350°F (175°C).

Carefully fry the mozzarella sticks in batches until they're golden brown, usually around 1-2 minutes.

Remove them from the oil and place them on paper towels to drain excess oil.

Serve hot with marinara sauce for dipping.

Nutritional values :

The nutritional content can vary based on the size, brand of ingredients used, and the cooking method. However, here's an approximate breakdown per serving (usually around 3-4 sticks):

1—Calories: Around 300-400 calories

2—Fat: Approximately 20-25 grams

3–Protein: Roughly 15-20 grams: About 15-20 grams.

4—Sodium: Varies based on ingredients and portion size, but can be moderate to high due to cheese and seasoning.

These values can change based on factors like portion size, specific ingredients, or variations in the cooking process. Enjoy these delicious treats in moderation as they tend to be high in calories and fat due to the frying process and cheese content.

3–LOADED POTATO CHIPS

Loaded potato skins are a popular appetizer or snack made from hollowed-out potato halves, filled with a savoury mixture of cheese, bacon, sour cream, and green onions. They are baked until the cheese is melted and bubbly, resulting in a deliciously indulgent treat.

Mode of Preparation:
Ingredients:

Russet potatoes
Cooking oil (such as olive oil)   Salt
Pepper
Shredded cheddar cheese
Cooked and crumbled bacon 9 Sour cream

Chopped green onions

<u>Preparation Steps:</u>
Preheat the oven to 400°F (200°C).   Scrub
the potatoes thoroughly and pat them dry.
Pierce the potatoes several times with a fork and rub
them with oil, salt, and pepper. Place the potatoes
directly on the oven rack or a baking sheet lined with foil
and bake for about 45-60 minutes until they are tender
inside.

Once cooled slightly, cut the potatoes in half lengthwise and scoop out most of the flesh, leaving about ¼ inch attached to the skin. Brush the insides and outsides of the potato skins with oil and place them back in the oven for 10-15 minutes until they become crispy. Remove the potato skins from the oven and fill each with shredded cheese and bacon. Return the filled skins to the oven until the cheese melts and starts to bubble.Garnish with dollops of sour cream and chopped green onions before serving.

Nutritional Values

The nutritional content can vary based on the size of the potatoes, the amount of cheese and toppings used, and specific brands of ingredients.
Here is a layout per serving (typically around 2-3 potato halves):.

Calories: Around 200-300 calories
Fat: Approximately 10-15 grams
Protein: Roughly 8-12 grams
Carbohydrates: About 15-20 grams
Sodium: Varies based on ingredients,but can be moderate to high due to cheese and bacon. These values are estimates and may vary based on portion size and ingredients used. Loaded potato skins are delicious but can be calorie-dense due to cheese and bacon, so enjoy them in moderation. Adding more

vegetables or opting for lower-fat toppings can make them slightly healthier.

MINI PIZZAS

Mini pizzas are bite-sized versions of the classic pizza, typically made using small rounds of dough topped with sauce, cheese, and assorted toppings. They are versatile, customizable, and perfect for parties, snacks, or appetizers.

Mode of Preparation:

Ingredients: Pizza dough (store-bought or homemade) Pizza sauce or marinara sauce Shredded mozzarella cheese

Toppings of your choice (pepperoni, bell peppers, onions, mushrooms, olives, etc.) Olive oil

Italian seasoning (optional)

Preparation Steps:

Preheat the oven to the temperature recommended for the pizza dough (usually around 400-450°F or 200-230°C).

Roll out the pizza dough on a floured surface and cut it into smaller rounds using a cookie cutter or a small bowl. Place the dough rounds on a baking sheet lined with parchment paper. Spread a spoonful of pizza sauce on each dough round, leaving a small border around the edges.

Sprinkle shredded mozzarella cheese over the sauce.

Add your desired toppings evenly over the cheese. Drizzle a bit of olive oil around the edges of the dough for a golden crust and sprinkle with Italian seasoning if desired.   Bake in the preheated oven for about 10-12 minutes or until the crust is golden and the cheese is bubbly and melted.

Remove from the oven and let them cool for a few minutes before serving.

Nutritional Values:

The nutritional content of mini pizzas can vary depending on the type and amount of toppings used, the dough recipe, and portion sizes.

The breakdown per mini pizza (based on a standard size with cheese and basic toppings):

*Calories: Around 100-150 calories per mini pizza
*Fat: Approximately 4-8 grams
*Protein: Roughly 4-6 grams
*Carbohydrates: About 10-15 grams.
*Sodium: Varies based on toppings and cheese, but typically moderate

These values are estimates and can change significantly based on the chosen toppings and the size of the mini pizzas. To make them healthier, consider using whole wheat dough, leaner protein toppings, and plenty of vegetable options. Control portions to enjoy these delicious treats without consuming excessive calories.

CHAPTER THREE

QUICK AND HEALTHY MEALS

1- CHICKEN TENDERS

Preparation:

Cut chicken breasts into strips.

In a bowl, mix breadcrumbs, paprika, garlic powder, salt, and pepper.   Dip chicken strips into beaten egg, then coat with the breadcrumb mixture.   Preheat the air fryer and cook the tenders for 10-12 minutes, flipping halfway through.

Nutritional Values:

Chicken tenders are high in protein. Adjust the breadcrumb coating for a healthier option (whole wheat breadcrumbs or almond meal).

2–VEGGIE STIR FRY

Preparation:

Chop assorted veggies (bell peppers, broccoli, carrots, etc.).

Heat sesame oil in a pan, add minced garlic and ginger.

Stir in the veggies and cook until slightly tender. Add soy sauce or a light stir-fry sauce and cook for a few more minutes.

Nutritional Values:

High in vitamins, fibre, and antioxidants. Use minimal oil for a healthier dish.

3. QUINOA STUFFED PEPPERS

Preparation:

Cook quinoa according to package instructions. Cut the tops off bell peppers, remove seeds, and blanch in boiling water.   Mix cooked quinoa with black beans, corn, diced tomatoes, and seasoning.

Stuff peppers with the quinoa mixture and bake in the air fryer until peppers are tender.

Nutritional Values:

Quinoa provides protein and fibre.   Peppers are packed with vitamin C and other nutrients.

4. SALMON FILLETS

Preparation:

Season salmon fillets with salt, pepper, and your choice of herbs (dill, thyme, etc.). Preheat the air fryer and place the fillets in the basket.

Cook for about 8-10 minutes until the salmon is cooked through.

Nutritional Values:

Rich in omega-3 fatty acids and high-quality protein.

A heart-healthy option.

These recipes offer a variety of flavours, nutrients, and are relatively quick to prepare, making them ideal for young chefs looking for healthy meals. Adjustments can be made to suit individual dietary preferences and health goals.

CHAPTER FOUR

DELICIOUS DESSERTS

1–AIR FRIED DONUTS:
Preparation:

Mix flour, sugar, baking powder, salt, and nutmeg in a bowl.

Add milk, melted butter, and vanilla extract to form a dough.

Roll out the dough and use a donut cutter to shape them.

Air fry the donuts until golden brown. Optionally, coat them in cinnamon sugar or glaze once cooled.

Nutritional Values:

These homemade donuts can be lower in calories compared to deep-fried versions. Control sugar and fat content by adjusting ingredients.

2– CHOCOLATE CHIP COOKIES

Preparation:

Cream butter and sugar together until light and fluffy.

Add eggs and vanilla extract, then mix in flour, baking soda, and salt.

Stir in chocolate chips.

Scoop dough onto a lined air fryer basket and bake until golden.

Nutritional Values:

Cookies are high in sugar and fat.   Use dark chocolate chips or reduce sugar for a slightly healthier option.

3. APPLE CRISPS

Preparation:

Slice apples and toss with lemon juice,sugar, cinnamon, and a touch of flour.   In another bowl, mix oats, flour, sugar, cinnamon, and cold butter to form a crumbly topping.

Layer the apple mixture in a baking dish, top with the oat mixture, and air fry until bubbly and golden.

Nutritional Values:

Apples provide fibre and vitamins. Control added sugar and use whole-grain oats for a healthier crisp.

4–BERRY HAND PIES

Preparation:.

Roll out pie crust dough and cut into small circles. Mix berries with sugar and a bit of cornstarch. Place berry mixture onto half of each dough circle, fold over, and crimp edges. Air fry the hand pies until golden brown.

Nutritional Values:.

Berries are rich in antioxidants and vitamins. Opt for whole wheat or reduced-fat pie crust for a slightly healthier option.

These dessert recipes offer a variety of sweet treats that can be made in an air fryer. While desserts tend to be higher in sugar and fat, adjustments can be made to create slightly healthier versions by controlling ingredients and portions.

CHAPTER FIVE

FUN AND CREATIVE RECIPES

1–TACO CUPS

Taco cups are mini taco-like appetizers made by pressing tortillas into muffin tins to create a cup shape, then filling them with seasoned meat, cheese, and toppings like lettuce, tomatoes, and salsa.

Preparation:

1–Cut tortillas into circles slightly larger than the muffin tin openings.   2–Press the tortilla circles into the greased muffin tin to form cups.

3–Bake until they are crispy.   4–Cook seasoned ground meat (usually   beef or chicken) and fill the cups.   5–Add cheese and bake until melted.   6–Top with your favourite taco toppings.   Nutritional values can vary based on ingredients used, but generally, they're moderate in calories, with protein from the meat, some carbs from the tortillas, and various nutrients from the toppings.It is essential to watch portions and choose lean meats and healthier toppings for a balanced snack or meal.

2–CHICKEN QUESADILLAS Chicken quesadillas are a delicious Mexican dish made by placing a filling of cooked chicken, cheese, and sometimes other ingredients like onions, peppers, or salsa between two tortillas. The tortillas are then grilled or pan-fried until crispy and the cheese melts, creating a gooey, flavorful filling. They are usually served with sides like guacamole, sour cream, or salsa for dipping. It is a versatile dish that allows for various ingredient combinations and can be customized to suit different tastes.

To prepare chicken quesadillas: 1–Cook diced chicken breast in a pan with your preferred seasoning until fully cooked. 2–Lay a tortilla flat, sprinkle cheese over half of it, add the cooked chicken, and any other desired ingredients like sautéed onions, bell peppers, or salsa. 3–Fold the tortilla in half to cover the filling. 4–Cook the quesadilla in a skillet or on a griddle over medium heat until both sides are golden brown and the cheese is melted. Nutritional values can vary based on ingredients and portion sizes, but generally, chicken quesadillas provide protein from the chicken, calcium and protein from the cheese, and carbs from the tortilla. Depending on the cooking method and additional ingredients, they can range from moderate to higher in calories, so it's essential to use lean chicken, whole grain tortillas, and control portions for a healthier option. Adding vegetables like peppers or onions can also boost the nutritional value.

3–VEGGIE SPRING ROLLS

Veggie spring rolls are a popular Vietnamese dish made with rice paper wrappers filled with a variety of fresh vegetables like lettuce, carrots, cucumber, bell peppers, herbs like mint or basil, and sometimes vermicelli noodles or tofu. These rolls are often served with a dipping sauce like peanut sauce or a sweet chilli sauce. They are eaten cd and are known for their light, refreshing taste and crunchy texture from the fresh vegetables.

Preparation:

Prepare Fillings: Julienne or finely slice assorted vegetables like carrots, cucumbers, bell peppers, lettuce, and any other preferred veggies.

1–**Soak Wrappers**: Dip rice paper wrappers briefly in warm water to soften them.   2–**Assemble**:
Lay a softened wrapper flat, place a small amount of each vegetable filling in the centre, fold the sides in, and roll it tightly, like a burrito.

Nutritional Values: Spring rolls are generally low in calories, particularly when filled mainly with vegetables.   They are rich in vitamins, minerals, and dietary fibre from the veggies. The rice paper wrapper contributes carbohydrates but is relatively low in fat.

4–CUSTOMIZABLE AIR FRIED PIZZAS.

Preparation: 1–**Prepare Ingredients**: Gather pizza toppings like shredded cheese, marinara sauce, diced vegetables, meats, and any desired seasonings. 2–**Prepare Pizza Crust:** Use pre-made pizza dough or flatten out a portion of dough to the desired thickness. 3–**Assemble Pizzas:**   Spread marinara sauce over the dough, add toppings, then place it in the air fryer basket. 4–**Air Fry:** Cook the pizza in the air fryer until the crust is crispy and the cheese is melted.

Nutritional Values:

Nutritional values will vary based on toppings and crust. Using whole wheat or cauliflower crust can add more fibre and nutrients compared to traditional crusts. Load up on vegetables as toppings for added vitamins and minerals.   Using lean meats and limiting cheese can help keep calories and fat in check. Both recipes offer versatility and room for customization while being relatively healthy. They provide an opportunity to incorporate plenty of vegetables and control the amount of fat depending on the chosen ingredients.

CHAPTER SIX

TIPS FOR EXPERIMENTING

1–Creating Your Own Recipes;

Creating your own recipes can be   incredibly rewarding and allows   for culinary exploration.

1.Start with a Base:.

Choose a Core Ingredient: Begin with one main ingredient or dish you enjoy or are familiar with. It could be a protein (chicken, tofu, beans) or a base (pasta, rice, quinoa).   2.
Understand Flavors and Combinations: *Flavour Pairings: Learn about flavour profiles and which ingredients complement each other. Experiment with sweet, salty,   sour, bitter, and umami tastes.

*Balanced Seasoning:** Understand the balance of seasoning, such as using herbs, spices, acids (like lemon juice or vinegar), and oils.

3. Experiment Gradually:

*__Small Changes__: Start by making small changes to existing recipes. Modify one or two elements at a time (e.g., changing spices, adding a new vegetable, or altering cooking times).

*__Keep Notes:__ Document your changes, both successful and unsuccessful ones. This helps in understanding what worked and what did not. So that when you are preparing a recipe,you can improve your past experiences.

4. Texture and Visual Appeal:

*__Play with Textures:__ Incorporate different textures (crispy, creamy, chewy) to add depth to your dish.

*__Visual Presentation:__ Consider the visual appeal of the dish. Experiment with plating techniques and colourful ingredients for better taste and delight.

5.Do not fear Mistakes.

*__Embrace Failures:__ Not every experiment will result in a perfect dish. Mistakes often lead to learning and discovering new flavour combinations.

*__Adjust and Adapt:__ If something does not work the way you expected, do not be afraid to adjust or tweak the recipe until it matches your taste.

6. Taste as You Go:

*Frequent Tasting: Taste your dish throughout the cooking process. Adjust seasoning or ingredients as needed to achieve the desired flavour profile. Make it moderate,not low in taste nor too tasty but the desired state.

7. Seek Inspiration:

*Research and Explore: Gather inspiration from cookbooks, online recipes, food blogs, or cultural cuisines. Use them as a starting point for your own creations.

8. Share and Gather Feedback:

Get Feedback: Share your creations with friends or family and ask for their opinions. Constructive feedback can help refine your recipe.

9. Document and Refine:

***Write Down Changes:** Keep a detailed log of your recipes, modifications, and outcomes. This will help refine your recipes for future use. Do not hesitate to revisit and revise your recipes based on feedback and personal preferences.Creating your own recipes is an exciting journey that allows for personal expression and creativity in the kitchen. It is a process that involves exploration, experimentation, and the joy of discovering new flavours and dishes.

2-FLAVOUR PAIRING IDEAS:Flavour pairing is an art that enhances the taste and depth of your dishes.
1.Classic   Combo:

***Herbs and Proteins**: Rosemary with lamb, basil with tomatoes and mozzarella, or cilantro with fish.

***Sweet and Savory:** Honey with goat cheese, apples with cheddar, or bacon with maple syrup.

2. Global Fusion: *Asian Fusion: Soy sauce with ginger and garlic, lemongrass with coconut milk, or sesame with soy and honey.

*__Mediterranean Influence__: Olive oil with lemon and oregano, mint with yoghurt, or garlic with tahini.

3. Contrasting Tastes:

*__Balanced Contrasts:__ Pair sweet and spicy, like mango with chilli, or salty with sweet, such as prosciutto with melon.

*__Acidic and Creamy:__ Use balsamic vinegar with creamy cheese, or citrus with rich meats like duck.

4. Texture Combinations:

*__Crunch and Creamy__: Incorporate crunchy nuts with creamy sauces or salads, like almonds with a velvety pumpkin soup.

*Smooth and Chunky: Purees or smooth sauces paired with chunky salsas or relishes create an interesting textural contrast.

5. Seasonal and Local Pairings:

*__Seasonal Produce__: Combine ingredients that are in season for the freshest flavours and optimal pairings.

*__Local Specialties__: Experiment with local specialties or regional cuisines to discover unique flavour marriages.

*__Spice Blends:__ Create your own spice blends by mixing complementary spices. For instance, cumin with coriander and paprika or cinnamon with cloves.

7. Layering Flavours:

*__Building Layers__: Start with a base flavour (like garlic), add a contrasting note (like citrus), and finish with a hint of freshness (like herbs).

8. Beverage Pairings:

*__Cooking with Alcohol:__ Incorporate wine, beer, or spirits in cooking. For example, red wine with red meat or beer in batters for fried foods.

*__Tea and Infusions__: Use teas or infusions as a marinade or in sauces, like using green tea for poaching fish.

9- Dessert Innovations:

*Unexpected Sweetness: Experiment with sweet elements in savoury dishes, like adding fruit to salads or glazes for meats.

10**. Cultural Inspirations:**

*Ethnic Flavours: Explore various cuisines to understand their traditional pairings and adapt them to your recipes.

By exploring these diverse flavour combinations and experimenting with various ingredients, you can create unique, well-balanced, and delightful dishes that suit your palate and culinary preferences.

3–ADJUSTING COOKING TIME AND TEMPERATURE

Adjusting cook times and temperatures can be an art when it comes to achieving the perfect dish.

Factors to Consider:

1–Ingredients: Different foods have varying moisture content, density, and composition, influencing their cooking requirements. Thicker cuts or larger quantities may need more time, while delicate items might need less.

2–Cooking Method: Whether you're baking, frying, grilling, or using other methods, each technique has its optimal temperature and duration. Adjustments are needed based on the method employed. 3–Appliances: Different ovens, stovetops, and cooking gadgets may have slight variations in temperature accuracy. Familiarize yourself with your specific appliance's nuances.

TIPS FOR ADJUSTING

1–Start with Guidelines: Use standard recipes or guidelines as a base but be willing to deviate based on your experience and understanding of the dish.

2–Temperature Adjustments: Lower temperatures allow for slower, more even cooking, which can be great for tougher cuts of meat or delicate pastries. Higher temperatures can be ideal for crisping or searing. **3–Time Adjustments:** Monitor the food closely as it cooks. If it is cooking too quickly or slowly, make adjustments accordingly. Use visual cues (browning, bubbling) and internal temperature (using a thermometer) as indicators.

4–Preparation Changes: Altering the size, shape, or thickness of ingredients can influence cooking times. For instance, thinner slices will cook faster than thicker ones.

5–Resting Periods: Remember that some dishes continue to cook even after being removed from the heat source. Allowing food to rest before serving can affect its final texture and temperature.

6–Keep Notes: Record your adjustments and the results achieved. This will help refine your cooking process for future attempts.

7–Safety Precautions: While experimenting, ensure that food safety guidelines are still followed. Use a food thermometer to check that meats reach safe internal temperatures.

EXPERIMENTING MINDSET

1–Be Patient: Adjustments might take a few tries to get right. Don't get discouraged if the first attempt is not perfect.

2–Be Curious: Embrace the learning process. Each adjustment teaches something new about the cooking process and your preferences.

3–Taste Along the Way: Regularly taste your dish as it cooks to gauge flavour development and adjust seasoning if necessary.

FINAL THOUGHTS:

Experimenting with cook times and temperatures is about finding the balance between following a recipe and adapting it to suit your taste and cooking environment.
It is an opportunity to personalize dishes and refine your culinary skills. Trust your instincts, stay curious, and enjoy the journey of creating delicious meals!

CONCLUSION

It is an awesome experience diving into the world of culinary artistry with air fryer cooking methods.It is indeed a remarkable journey! As a young chef, your exploration with this modern kitchen marvel has been nothing short of awe-inspiring. From the first crispy, golden batch to the perfected dishes that followed, each creation speaks volumes about your dedication, creativity, and passion for cooking.

The air fryer, a vessel of culinary innovation, has been your faithful companion through experimenting with flavours, textures, and techniques. It's witnessed the fusion of ingredients and the birth of dishes that bear your signature touch. From classic fries to exotic delicacies, your air fryer has been the canvas upon which your imagination has painted delicious masterpieces.

This journey signifies more than just the culinary prowess you've honed; it symbolizes your willingness to embrace new technologies, techniques, and tools in your quest for culinary excellence. Your commitment to learning, adapting, and pushing the boundaries of traditional cooking methods showcases your growth as a chef.

May this journey with your air fryer continue to inspire your culinary adventures, encouraging you to explore new recipes, create innovative flavours, and share your delectable creations with the world. Your dedication as a young chef is admirable, and your air fryer has undoubtedly been a pivotal element in this flavorful expedition. Cheers to your culinary journey and the delightful dishes yet to come!

FINAL TIPS FOR YOUNG CHEFS

Below are some concluding tips for young chefs venturing into the culinary world:

1–Experiment Fearlessly: Do not be afraid to try new ingredients, techniques, or flavour combinations. Cooking is an art, and your kitchen is your canvas.

2–Master the Basics: Before diving into complex recipes, ensure you have a solid foundation in basic cooking techniques. It will serve as a springboard for your culinary creativity.

3–Taste as You Go: Constantly taste your dishes while cooking. Adjust seasoning and flavours as needed throughout the process; it is easier to fix along the way than at the end.

4–Organization is Key: Keep your workspace tidy and organized. This not only streamlines your cooking process but also makes it safer and more enjoyable.

5–**Learn from Mistakes:** Do not be discouraged by failures; they are stepping stones to success. Embrace them, learn from them, and grow as a chef.

6–Creativity and Adaptability: Be open to improvisation and change. Sometimes the best dishes come from a little experimentation and adaptation.

7–Respect Ingredients: Use fresh, quality ingredients and respect their flavours. Let them shine in your dishes rather than overpowering them with excessive seasonings or techniques.

8–Time Management: Develop good time management skills in the kitchen. Plan your recipes, prepare ingredients beforehand, and group tasks efficiently.

9–Seek Inspiration: Constantly seek inspiration from various cuisines, chefs, cookbooks, and cultural dishes. It broadens your culinary horizons.

10–Share Your Experience: Whether it is with family, friends, or a wider audience, share your love for cooking. Food brings people together, and your creations can spark joy in others.

Remember that the kitchen is your playground. Have fun, be passionate, and let your love for food reflect in every dish you create.

Thank you dear reader for taking your time to read through this Cookbook. Kindly drop a review for me. I believe that the contents have greatly metamorphosed your culinary art. Thank you!

Printed in Great Britain
by Amazon

38500943R00056